Ten P
about F

ex libris

Candlestick Press

Published by:
Candlestick Press,
Diversity House, 72 Nottingham Road, Arnold, Nottingham NG5 6LF
www.candlestickpress.co.uk

Design and typesetting by Craig Twigg

Printed by Ratcliff & Roper Print Group, Nottinghamshire, UK

Selection and Introduction © Katharine Towers, 2020

Cover illustration © Angie Lewin, 2020
www.angielewin.co.uk

Candlestick Press monogram © Barbara Shaw, 2008

© Candlestick Press, 2020

ISBN 978 1 907598 87 6

Acknowledgements:

The poems in this pamphlet are reprinted from the following books, all by
permission of the publishers listed unless stated otherwise. Every effort has
been made to trace the copyright holders of the poems published in this book.
The editor and publisher apologise if any material has been included without
permission or without the appropriate acknowledgement, and would be glad to be
told of anyone who has not been consulted.

Thanks are due to all the copyright holders cited below for their kind permission:

Beth Davies, *Wild Poetry* (Hive South Yorkshire, 2017) by kind permission of
the author. Helen Dunmore, *Counting Backwards: Poems 1975-2017* (Bloodaxe
Books, 2019) www.bloodaxebooks.com. John Heath-Stubbs, *Collected Poems*
(Carcanet Press, 1988) by kind permission of David Higham Associates. Seán
Hewitt, *Lantern* (Offord Road Books, 2019), by permission of poet and publisher.
Mimi Khalvati, *New and Selected Poems* (Carcanet Press, 2007). Anne Ridler,
Collected Poems (Carcanet Press, 1997).

All permissions cleared courtesy of Swift Permissions
swiftpermissions@gmail.com

Where poets are no longer living their dates are given.

Introduction

The advertising slogan 'Say it with flowers' was first used in America on Mother's Day in 1918. Major Patrick O'Keefe of Boston coined the phrase (which he never copyrighted) and which soon became popular around the world. Beth Davies' 'Floriography' which closes this selection of flower poems explores and expands on the Victorian fascination with the language of flowers. In the nineteenth century, carefully selected floral arrangements became a way of communicating in code – particularly useful for secret lovers.

When choosing these ten poems I wanted to create a beautiful bouquet that would speak eloquently to all manner of occasions. The selection encompasses ageing, religious devotion, the delights of the senses, being surprised by pure joy and the rewards of paying attention to small things. And, of course, there is love.

As the poems demonstrate, flowers can be recruited to express all sorts of human emotions and experiences. For Wordsworth, the common daisy is a lesson in humility while for Helen Dunmore, lilacs growing on a city street or a motorway roundabout demonstrate generosity by releasing "their sweet, wild perfume" even in the midst of urban grubbiness. DH Lawrence's passionate and mysterious celebration of gentians is a glorious, visionary rhapsody. In his poem, the repeated word 'blue' becomes a sort of spell.

That the poems range over three centuries is testament to poetry's abiding fascination with the essence and beauty of the world of flowers. There will, surely, never be a time when the last poem about a rose has been written! That flowers always manage to hold back something that cannot quite be grasped in words is part of their enduring allure.

Katharine Towers

Waterlily

glory be to the *näckros*, naked rose,
open rose, white flower of water.

glory be to water, held in dropped-
stone-ripple, thickened to the green

pad of a leaf. & in time
let us praise the spread

of all anchored things.
praise to the long pale roots

& the chain of water. & let us
take this flower, its quiet face

on the surface & its searching
root as the mystery of faith.

glory be to the work of the pond
& to silt, to the white

open flower which is an offering
& will be given up for us.

Seán Hewitt

Overblown Roses

She held one up, twirling it in her hand
as if to show me how the world began
and ended in perfection. I was stunned.
How could she make a rose so woebegone,
couldn't silk stand stiff? And how could a child,
otherwise convinced of her mother's taste,
know what to think? *It's overblown*, she smiled,
I love roses when they're past their best.

'Overblown roses', the words rang in my head,
making sense as I suddenly saw afresh
the rose now, the rose ahead: where a petal
clings to a last breath; where my mother's flesh
and mine, going the same way, may still
be seen as beautiful, if these words are said.

Mimi Khalvati

Celandine

Thinking of her had saddened me at first,
Until I saw the sun on the celandines lie
Redoubled, and she stood up like a flame,
A living thing, not what before I nursed,
The shadow I was growing to love almost,
The phantom, not the creature with bright eye
That I had thought never to see, once lost.

She found the celandines of February
Always before us all. Her nature and name
Were like those flowers, and now immediately
For a short swift eternity back she came,
Beautiful, happy, simply as when she wore
Her brightest bloom among the winter hues
Of all the world; and I was happy too,
Seeing the blossoms and the maiden who
Had seen them with me Februarys before,
Bending to them as in and out she trod
And laughed, with locks sweeping the mossy sod.

But this was a dream: the flowers were not true,
Until I stooped to pluck from the grass there
One of five petals and I smelt the juice
Which made me sigh, remembering she was no more,
Gone like a never perfectly recalled air.

Edward Thomas (1878 – 1917)

Bavarian Gentians

Not every man has gentians in his house
in soft September, at slow, sad Michaelmas.

Bavarian gentians, big and dark, only dark
darkening the day-time, torch-like with the smoking blueness of
   Pluto's gloom,
ribbed and torch-like, with their blaze of darkness spread blue
down flattening into points, flattened under the sweep of white day
torch-flower of the blue-smoking darkness, Pluto's dark-blue daze,
black lamps from the halls of Dis, burning dark blue,
giving off darkness, blue darkness, as Demeter's pale lamps give off light,
lead me then, lead the way.

Reach me a gentian, give me a torch!
let me guide myself with the blue, forked torch of this flower
down the darker and darker stairs, where blue is darkened on blueness,
even where Persephone goes, just now, from the frosted September
to the sightless realm where darkness is awake upon the dark
and Persephone herself is but a voice
or a darkness invisible enfolded in the deeper dark
of the arms Plutonic, and pierced with the passion of dense gloom,
among the splendour of torches of darkness, shedding darkness on
   the lost bride and her groom.

DH Lawrence (1885 – 1930)

Inscription for a Scented Garden for the Blind

Wayfarer, pause. Although you may not see,
Earth's bright children, herbs and flowers, are here:
It is their small essential souls that greet you,
Mounted upon the morning or evening air:
While from above, from sky and tree-bough,
Birds fling down their songs, a musical burgeoning.

John Heath-Stubbs (1918 – 2006)

To the Daisy

With little here to do or see
Of things that in the great world be,
Daisy! again I talk to thee,
   For thou art worthy,
Thou unassuming Common-place
Of Nature, with that homely face,
And yet with something of a grace,
   Which Love makes for thee!

Oft on the dappled turf at ease
I sit, and play with similes,
Loose types of things through all degrees,
   Thoughts of thy raising:
And many a fond and idle name
I give to thee, for praise or blame,
As is the humour of the game,
   While I am gazing.

A nun demure of lowly port;
Or sprightly maiden, of Love's court,
In thy simplicity the sport
   Of all temptations;
A queen in crown of rubies drest;
A starveling in a scanty vest;
Are all, as seems to suit thee best,
   Thy appellations.

A little Cyclops with one eye
Staring to threaten and defy,
That thought comes next – and instantly
   The freak is over,
The shape will vanish – and behold
A silver shield with boss of gold,
That spreads itself, some faery bold
   In fight to cover!

I see thee glittering from afar –
And then thou art a pretty star;
Not quite so fair as many are
   In heaven above thee!
Yet like a star, with glittering crest,
Self-poised in air thou seem'st to rest; –
May peace come never to his nest,
   Who shall reprove thee!

Bright *Flower*! for by that name at last,
When all my reveries are past,
I call thee, and to that cleave fast,
   Sweet silent creature!
That breath'st with me in sun and air,
Do thou, as thou art wont, repair
My heart with gladness, and a share
   Of thy meek nature!

William Wordsworth (1770 – 1850)

The Ragwort

Ragwort, thou humble flower with tattered leaves,
I love to see thee come and litter gold
What time the summer binds her russet sheaves,
Decking rude spots in beauties manifold,
That without thee were dreary to behold,
Sunburnt and bare – the meadow bank, the baulk
That leads a wagon-way through mellow fields
Rich with the tints that harvest's plenty yields,
Browns of all hues; and everywhere I walk
Thy waste of shining blossoms richly shields
The sun-tanned sward in splendid hues that burn
So bright and glaring that the very light
Of the rich sunshine doth to paleness turn,
And seems but very shadows in thy sight.

John Clare (1793 – 1864)

Snakeshead Fritillaries

Some seedlings shoulder the earth away
Like Milton's lion plunging to get free,
Demanding notice. Delicate rare fritillary,
You enter creeping, like the snake
You're named for, and lay your ear to the ground.
The soundless signal comes, to arch the neck –
Losing the trampled look –
Follow the code for colour, whether
White or freckled with purple and pale,
A chequered dice-box tilted over the soil,
The yellow dice held at the base.

When light slants before the sunset, this is
The proper time to watch fritillaries.
They entered creeping; you go on your knees,
The flowers level with your eyes,
And catch the dapple of sunlight through the petals.

Anne Ridler (1912 – 2001)

City lilacs

In crack-haunted alleys, overhangs,
plots of sour earth that pass for gardens,
in the space between wall and wheelie bin,

where men with mobiles make urgent conversation,
where bare-legged girls shiver in April winds,
where a new mother stands on her doorstep and blinks
at the brightness of morning, so suddenly born –

in all these places the city lilacs are pushing
their cones of blossom into the spring
to be taken by the warm wind.

Lilac, like love, makes no distinction.
It will open for anyone.
Even before love knows that it is love
lilac knows it must blossom.

In crack-haunted alleys, in overhangs,
in somebody's front garden
abandoned to crisp packets and cans,

on landscaped motorway roundabouts,
in the depth of parks
where men and women are lost in transactions
of flesh and cash, where mobiles ring

and the deal is done – here the city lilacs
release their sweet, wild perfume
then bow down, heavy with rain.

Helen Dunmore (1952 – 2017)

Floriography

Like me, they were afraid
of how words bloom between
people. They preferred the silence
of a bouquet left on a doorstep, a heart
worn in a buttonhole. They understood

what I don't: the significance
of a carnation's shade, the melancholy
of a red geranium in a left hand,
how orange lilies know as much of hatred
as fists do, the bittersweet of nightshade

and truth. Is there a flower
for the wordless poetry trapped
in my chest? If I pressed petals
between these pages, would you know
what I am trying to say?

Beth Davies

*Floriography, or the language of flowers, was popular in
Victorian times. Each plant had a meaning associated with it, so
that a wide variety of sentiments could be expressed by giving
someone flowers.*